Healthy Choices

STAYING SAFE OUTSIDE AND ONLINE

By R. J. MacReady

Cavendish Square
New York

Published in 2022 by Cavendish Square Publishing, LLC
243 5th Avenue, Suite 136, New York, NY 10016

First Edition

Library of Congress Cataloging-in-Publication Data

Names: MacReady, R. J., author.
Title: Staying safe outside and online / R. J. MacReady.
Description: New York : Cavendish Square Publishing, [2022] | Series: Healthy choices | Includes index.
Identifiers: LCCN 2020034891 | ISBN 9781502659767 (library binding) | ISBN 9781502659743 (paperback) | ISBN 9781502659750 (set) | ISBN 9781502659774 (ebook)
Subjects: LCSH: Outdoor recreation for children–Safety measures–Juvenile literature. | Internet and children–Safety measures–Juvenile literature.
Classification: LCC GV191.625 .M33 2022 | DDC 796.5028/9–dc23
LC record available at https://lccn.loc.gov/2020034891

Editor: Greg Roza
Designer: Andrea Davison-Bartolotta

The photographs in this book are used by permission and through the courtesy of: Cover Tom Wang/Shutterstock.com; p. 5 (top left) Will & Deni McIntyre/Corbis Documentary/Getty Images; p. 5 (top right) Rebecca Nelson/The Image Bank/Getty Images; p. 5 (bottom left) Fresh Meat Media LLC/The Image Bank/Getty Images Plus/Getty Images; p. 5 (bottom right) blackCAT/E+/Getty Images; p. 7 Morsa Images/DigitalVision/Getty Images; p. 9 Enrico Calderoni/Getty Images; p. 11 mkitina4/iStock/Getty Images Plus/Getty Images; p. 13 Stock Rocket/Shutterstock.com; p. 15 CasarsaGuru/E+/Getty Images; p. 17 pixdeluxe/E+/Getty Images; p. 19 anyaberkut/iStock/Getty Image Plus/Getty Images; p. 21 Valeriy_G/iStock/Getty Images Plus/Getty Images; p. 23 Nitat Termmee/Moment/Getty Images.

CPSIA compliance information: Batch #CW22CSQ: For further information contact Cavendish Square Publishing LLC, New York, New York, at 1-877-980-4450.

Printed in the United States of America

CONTENTS

Free Time!

What do you do in your free time? Some people play sports. Some people read. Others play video games online. No matter what you like to do, it's important to know how to make safe choices while having fun.

Let's Go Outside

Playing outside is good for your health. You can run and play games. You can go to a playground with friends. You can enjoy sunshine and fresh air! You should know how to stay safe when playing outside.

Manners are important. Always treat others kindly when you play. Talk kindly to others, and don't fight with them. Make sure everyone gets a chance to play. Taking turns is a healthy choice!

Sometimes people get hurt playing outside. Small **injuries** include cuts and **bruises**. Always be careful when playing with others. This can stop injuries from happening. If someone gets hurt, tell a trusted adult right away.

People you don't know are called strangers. Most strangers are good people. However, you should never talk to strangers when you're playing outside. Some strangers want to hurt others. Always tell a trusted adult if a stranger is bothering you.

Let's Go Online

Using the internet is a great way to learn new things. However, not all websites are truthful. Ask a trusted adult to help you go to websites, and let them know what you're doing online.

You may meet strangers online. Never share **personal** facts about yourself. Never post pictures of yourself for strangers to see. Tell a trusted adult if a stranger tries to talk to you online or asks you to meet them in person.

Some websites ask you to use a password. Keep your passwords secret! Only you and your parents should know it. Never use a password that someone could guess. Never use your own name. Never use your birthday.

username
****
login

Sometimes people download music, games, and pictures from the internet. This means the **files** are placed on your computer. Some people like to spread computer **viruses**. You can't trust every file. Ask a parent before downloading anything to your computer.

Whether you're playing outside or inside on the computer, it's important to make healthy choices. Don't talk to strangers. Make sure a trusted adult knows where you are and who you're with. Of course, have fun too!

WORDS TO KNOW

bruises: Dark spots on a person's skin where they were bumped or hit.

files: Ways computers store information. Files may be music, games, photos, and many other things.

injuries: Hurt or damage.

personal: Having to do with a specific person.

viruses: Files that can hurt your computer.

INDEX